All-new Amazon Fire HD 10 Tablet Manual

User Guide and Full Instructions for Fire HD 10 Tablet, 2021 Release (11th Generation

Steve Rufus

ISBN: 9798533126199

Contents

1. Features

- Octa-core processor 2.0GHz

- 3GB RAM

- 32 / 64GB storage memory

- SD card slot (up to 1TB)

- 1080p (1920 x 1200) 10.1-inch screen 224ppi

- Rear-facing camera 5MP

- Front-facing camera 2MP

- Recording video in 720p HD

- Enhanced aluminosilicate glass

- Wi-Fi 2.4GHz & 5.0GHz / Bluetooth 5.0 LE (A2DP support) connection

- 3.5mm headphone port (stereo)

- Built-in speakers

- Dolby Atmos

- 2 integrated microphones

- Works with Amazon Appstore

- Supports Microsoft Office, OneNote, DropBox, Zoom, Skype, etc.

- Fully hands-free with Alexa, Show Mode

- Supports split screen

- USB Type-C slot for charging (2.0 version)

- 6,300 mAh battery

- 4 hours charging time

- Ambient light sensor

- Accelerometer

- 9.73 x 6.53 x 0.36 inches

- Weighs 16.4oz

- Available in 4 colors: Black, Denim, Olive, Lavender

2. Package

The tablet is packed in a small orange cardboard box with the picture of the tablet and its name on the front, and a shortlist of features on the back. Pull at the protecting tape at the top on the back following the arrows' direction, and open the box.

Contents:

- a small cardboard rack with a compartment in the bottom part

- a tablet wrapped in plastic

- a USB-C charging cable

- an Amazon 9W power adapter with the US plug

- two orange-colored cards featuring the Quick Start Guide instructions on them.

3. Get Started

3.1 Examine the Tablet

The front part of the tablet, when viewed horizontally, has a display with a frame and a front camera eye in the middle of the top frame (if placed vertically, the front-facing camera will be on the left). Two sets of speaker holes (7 holes each) are closer to the corners on the top side.

The back cover features an Amazon logo in the center and a rear-facing camera eye in the top left corner. The back panel is soft non-slippery plastic, smooth to tap. The box's corners are rounded.

The microSD card slot with the rubber cap is located at the bottom. The tablet's connections are on the right side. From the top-down, it follows:

- a volume control button with a notch in the middle (pressing the top part of the button increases the volume, pressing the bottom part of the button decreases the volume)

- a Power button (long press to access the turn on/off menu; short press to activate the display after a period of inactivity)

- two microphone slots

- a USB-C slot for charging

- a 3.5mm stereo headphone port

3.2 Prepare Your Device

Before turning on the tablet, make sure it is fully charged.

Charge the Battery

1. Make sure the temperature isn't too hot or too cold. Extreme temperatures can damage the tablet and prevent it from charging. A humid environment and direct sunlight should be avoided.

2. Disconnect the power adapter from the outlet and the charging cable from the USB-C port (if it was plugged in).

3. Restart the tablet. Hold down the Power button for 40 seconds or until it restarts.

4. Connect the charging cable's USB-C connector to the tablet's USB-C port.

5. Connect the charging cable's USB-A connector to the power adapter, then plug the adapter into the outlet.

6. The tablet's indicator light turns amber, indicating that it is charging.

7. The charge indicator light turns green, indicating that the battery is fully charged.

4. Begin to Use Your Tablet

4.1 Lock or Unlock Your Device

1. Shortly press the Power button. The tablet's screen must be turned on.

2. Swipe up to the top of the screen to unlock it.

3. To lock the screen, press the Power button for a short time again.

By default, there's no additional unlock protection on the tablet. To prevent unauthorized access to your tablet, go to the Settings menu and set a password or PIN code.

4.2 How to Fix Possible Startup Issues

1. Make sure the tablet is fully charged. Before starting it, charge through the USB-C cable and the Amazon-branded adapter for at least 30 minutes. If you wait for the indicator to turn green earlier, it means that the tablet is fully charged. Disconnect the charger.

2. Turn off the tablet. Press the Power button for 40 seconds. If the Startup menu appears, continue to hold the button until the tablet turns off.

3. Turn the tablet on. Hold down the Power button until the screen lights up showing the Fire logo on it.

4.3 How to Restart Your Tablet

1. Press the Power button for 40 seconds or until the tablet shuts off. Then press and hold the Power button until the screen lights up.

2. Press the Power button for three seconds or until the shutdown message appears on the screen. Press "OK" to turn off the tablet. Then press and hold the Power button until the screen lights up.

4.4 How to Set Up Your Device

1. The first screen.

   - Select the language you'd like to operate the tablet with.

   - In order to make the font bigger or smaller, tap on the "aA" symbols at the bottom of the screen. The symbols are arranged from the smallest font size to the biggest.

   - If you need to scroll the list of languages, tap the screen with your finger and drag it to the top or to the bottom. The available languages are English (US), English (UK), English (Canada), German, Spanish, French, Italian, Japanese, Portuguese, and Chinese. For English (UK), German, Spanish, and French there are regional format options available.

   - To select the regional format, tap on the arrow in front of the language, and open the dropdown menu.

   - Tap on the desired language format.

- When the language or a regional format is selected, a tick icon appears next to it.

- After selecting the language, tap on the blue arrow in the bottom right corner.

2. The second screen shows the Wi-Fi networks available.

  - To refresh the list, tap on the rounded arrow in the top right corner.

  - Locate your home network or another Wi-Fi source on the list, and tap on its name.

  - If the Wi-Fi network is secured, the tablet will ask you to enter the password on the next display.

  - Tap on the field with "Password" on it and enter the password symbols on the virtual keyboard that appears at the bottom of the screen.

  - If you need to verify the password, tap on the empty box next to the Show password option beneath the field.

  - To access the advanced options, tap on the relevant box beneath it.

- In order to cancel connecting to the selected Wi-Fi network, tap the transparent CANCEL button in the bottom left corner.

- To continue with the selected Wi-Fi settings, tap on the blue CONTINUE button in the bottom right corner.

3. On the third screen, the Amazon account password should be entered.

   - Verify that the account's name matches yours. If not, tap on the blue Switch accounts inscription beneath.

   - If you forgot your password, tap on the blue "Forgot your password?" button.

   - Tap on the Password field and enter the Amazon account password on the virtual keyboard.

   - When everything is done, tap on the amber tick button on the keyboard.

4. On the fourth screen, the Fire options are listed.

- *Enable Location services*—allows the tablet to detect your location. Tap a box next to it to enable this option. A green tick should appear inside it. To disable this option, tap it one more time. Tap on the blue button beneath to find information about the Location Services.

- *Auto-Save Photos and Videos*—uploads your photo and video content to your Amazon Cloud drive by default. Tap a box next to it to enable this option. Tap on the blue button beneath to find information about the Auto-Save option. Tap the blue inscription next to it to access the list of options for this feature.

- *Save Wi-Fi Passwords to Amazon*—allows you to save the Wi-Fi passwords entered on your tablet and apply them to other Amazon devices. Tap on the blue button beneath to find more information about this option.

Tap the blue CONTINUE button in the bottom left corner.

5.   The Meet you Fire tablet inscription appears on the screen.

- The educational video starts.

- To forward/skip the video, tap and drag with your finger the blue dot on the playback line beneath the video.

6.   The Import profile screen appears.

- You must see your Amazon account name with the tick next to it that cannot be disabled.

- You can also tap on the plus button below and add a child or another profile. Tap on the blue CONTINUE button in the bottom right corner of the screen.

7. A Set Screen Lock screen appears.

- Select the PIN or password option, enter the code or the password on the virtual keyboard at the bottom, and tap on the amber tick symbol.

- Then, tap on the Confirm PIN or Confirm password field and enter the code or a password again.

- Tap on the blue CONTINUE button in the bottom right corner of the screen.

8. A Goodreads screen appears.

- You can log in or sign up for a Goodreads account. For that, tap on the blue CONTINUE button and proceed to the next screen.

- In order to skip this subscription, tap on the "NOT NOW" transparent button in the bottom left corner.

9. An Audible Plus screen appears.

- In order to go on with the Audible Plus subscription, tap on the yellow Start Your Free Trial button below.

- To skip this option, tap on the "No thanks" inscription next to it.

10. A Kindle Unlimited screen appears.

- To continue with the Kindle Unlimited subscription, tap on the yellow Start Your Free Trial button below.

- To skip this option, tap on the "No thanks" inscription next to it.

11. A Prime membership screen appears.

- You can tap the CONTINUE transparent button in the bottom right corner or skip this option by tapping on the NOT NOW button in the bottom right corner.

12. An Apps and Games for Free screen appears.

- You can tap the CONTINUE transparent button in the bottom right corner or skip this option by tapping on the NOT NO" button in the bottom right corner.

13. An Alexa screen appears.

- Tap on the blue CONTINUE button beneath.

- In order to activate Alexa, tap on the blue ENABLE ALEXA button on the right.

- In order to skip this option, tap on the transparent DISABLE ALEXA button on the left.

4.5 How to Set Up an Email Address

1. Swipe right or left to go to the Home screen.

2. Tap on the Email icon on the screen.

3. Enter your email address in the relevant field via the virtual keyboard at the bottom.

4. Tap on the NEXT button.

5. Enter your email account's password. Tap on the NEXT button.

6. Tap on the GO TO INBOX button to access your email box.

4.6 How to Transfer Data from an Old Fire Tablet

1. Delete any apps or content that you don't use from your old Fire tablet. Delete the relevant files and apps only if the progress within them isn't important to you, as deleted apps' progress isn't saved. Tap on and hold the app icon, then select the Delete from device option.

2. Turn on the Wi-Fi on your old tablet and Sync to the Cloud drive manually. Open the Settings menu from the Home screen or swipe down, go to Settings (via the gear icon), and toggle on the Sync box.

3. Swipe down from the top of the Home page and go to the Settings menu. Tap on the Device options and then proceed to Backup & restore. Enable the Backup option. This allows your tablet to make a weekly backup. The backed-up content includes:

   - bookmarks (for Silk browser)

   - Home page layout

   - personal settings

4.   If you have Amazon Drive, activate the Sync option to back up your photos and videos.

5.   Hook up your old Fire tablet to your computer via USB cable.

6.   In the computer OS, launch the Search program and detect the Kindle Fire folder. Open it.

7.   Create a separate folder on your computer's hard drive and give it a name.

8.   Copy and paste the non-system folders from the Kindle Fire folder into the newly created folder. You can copy the following folders:

- alarms

- documents

- pictures

- audible

- books

- music

- movies

- download

- android

9. Disconnect your old tablet from the computer.

10. Eject the microSD card (if any) from your old tablet.

11. Insert the microSD card into your new tablet.

12. Turn on the new tablet.

13. Tap on the Apps or games icon, and go to the settings.

14. Select the Cloud link and open the Cloud space.

15. For each app/game you wish to download from the Cloud, tap and hold on it until the pop-up menu appears. Select Download. Wait until the app/game is fully downloaded before going to the next one. Perform the same process with Books, Music, etc. content.

16. Connect your new Fire tablet to the computer.

17. Open two windows on the computer's display. The first window is for the new tablet, and the second is for the folder with previously saved files.

18. Saved files from the saved folders should be copied to the appropriate folders on your new tablet. If an overwriting warning displays, click to accept that the files in your new tablet folders will be overwritten.

The files with the wording "token" in their names are the exception.

19. Disconnect the new Fire tablet from the computer.

4.7 How to Transfer Content From Your Computer

1. If you've got a MAC computer, download and install the Android File Transfer program. If your PC runs on Windows OS, the necessary drivers are already preinstalled on it.

2. Connect your tablet to your computer using the USB-C cable.

3. Open the computer menu and look into the Drives section.

4. Locate the content on the tablet that you want to transfer and save it to a single folder on your computer.

5. Unlock the tablet screen.

6. Open the Fire device in the computer menu.

7. Go to the Internal storage folder and open it. (On a MAC OS, the Android FileTransfer opens the folder automatically after installation.)

8. Locate the appropriate folder within the Internal storage for the content you want to transfer. The audio files must be saved in the Music folder, the videos—in the Movies, etc.

9. Drag and drop content files from your computer's folders into the Fire tablet's internal storage folders.

10. Unplug the USB-C cable from your computer and the Fire tablet.

4.8 How to Find the User Guide

1. Swipe down from the top of the Home page.

2. Launch the settings by tapping the small gear in the bottom corner of the window (or go to the Settings menu on the Home page).

3. Select the Help option.

4. Tap on the User Guide icon.

4.9 How to Change the Screen Brightness

1. Swipe down from the top of the Home page.

2. Disclose the settings menu by tapping the small gear in the bottom corner of the window (or go to the Settings menu on the Home page).

3. Tap on the Display option.

4. Select the Brightness level menu.

5. Press and hold the slider while dragging forward and backward to brighten or darken the screen.

4.10 How to Change the Screen Timeout

1. Swipe down from the top of the Home page.

2. Open the Settings by tapping the small gear in the bottom corner of the window (or go to the Settings menu on the Home page).

3. Tap on the Display option.

4. Select the Sleep menu by tapping on it.

5. Tap on the circle next to the chosen timeout option. Available options are the following:

   - 15 seconds

   - 30 seconds

   - 1 minute

   - 2 minutes

   - 5 minutes

   - 10 minutes

   - 30 minutes

4.11 How to Turn the Volume Up and Down

1. Swipe down and tap on the gear icon or go to the Settings menu on the Home page. Proceed to the Sounds submenu. Tap and drag the amber slider on the screen. Drag to the left to reduce the volume, and drag to the right to increase it.

2. Press any of the volume controls a single time. Manipulate the slider as described in step 1.

3. Press and hold the upper volume button part to increase the volume, and the lower one to decrease it.

4.12 How to Set or Change the Time

1. On the tablet, turn on the Wi-Fi connection. Make sure that the signal is stable.

2. Swipe down and open the Settings menu (or from the Home page). Tap on the Device options submenu.

3. Select the Date & Time submenu.

4. If the box next to the Automatic time zone is empty, tap on it to put a tick there. Check the time reading at the top of the screen to see if it shows your local time.

5. If the Automatic time zone is activated, tap on the box to remove the tick. Wait 5 seconds before continuing. Tap on the box again to place a tick. Check the time reading at the top of the screen.

6. If the time reading doesn't correspond to your local time, disable the Automatic time zone, and select your time zone from the dropdown list.

7. You can set the time manually by tapping on the option Set time. Enter the hours and

minutes in two windows that appear and press the SAVE button.

4.13 How to Take Screenshots

1. Swipe up to unlock the tablet screen. Enter your PIN or Password, if required.

2. Open the app/document or go to the screen you want to capture.

3. Press simultaneously the Power button and Volume button down for 1 second. The screen should blink shortly and the screenshot miniature appears and moves to the top right corner of the screen.

4. On the Home screen, tap on the Photos app in order to view and edit the taken screenshot.

4.14 How to Use Camera

1. Tap on the camera app on the Home screen. The picture of the objects in front of the camera should appear on the screen.

2. Click on the area you want to focus on. The area should become more detailed.

3. Use your two fingers stretching or pinching on the screen in order to zoom in or out the picture. This can also be performed via pressing the Volume button down and up at the right-hand side.

4. To switch from the rear-facing camera to the front-facing camera, tap the reversing arrows icon at the top of the screen.

5. Tap the Gear icon in the top right corner of the screen to open the camera settings:

   - Enable/disable HDR

   - Image review options

   - Panoramic shooting

   - Lenticular shooting

6. For taking pictures:

- Tap on the Shutter icon to take a picture.

- Hold the Shutter icon to take several photos within seconds.

7. For recording videos:

- Tap on the camera icon.

- When you're ready to record, press the red Record button in the bottom right corner of the screen.

- Press the Stop button (it replaces the Record button when you start recording) in order to stop recording. You can press the Record button once more to make a new recording.

8. Tap on the Film icon at the bottom to open a strip of the photos and videos that have been taken recently.

4.15 How to Clear Browser History

1. To access Settings, swipe down and tap the Gear icon. Select the Apps & Notifications option.

2. Tap on Amazon Application Settings and find Silk Browser among the options. To access browser settings, tap on it.

3. Select the Clear Browser Data option from the Privacy submenu.

4. Tap on the boxes next to the types of data you want to delete. The boxes must be checked.

5. Hit the CLEAR DATA button.

4.16 How to Enable Split Screen

With a keyboard connected. To use Split Screen, hold down the keys "Fn" and "S" at the same time.

Without a keyboard:

1. On your tablet, open the apps you wish to see in Split Screen mode.

2. To open the Task Switcher and see the open apps in the list, tap on the Square icon at the bottom of the screen.

3. Tap the Menu icon in the top right corner of the app's preview and select the Split Screen option.

4. Tap on the preview of another app to add it to the Split Screen view.

Tip: To turn off the Split Screen view, tap and hold the edge of one of the apps' windows. To get a full-screen view, drag it to the right.

4.17 How to Install Software Updates

When your tablet connects to the internet, the following software updates are installed automatically:

- general system improvements

- features facilitating and speeding up the performance

If the automatic software updates do not install, use the following steps to manually download and install the latest updates:

1. Ascertain that your computer is equipped with the necessary software for transferring files to your tablet:

    - for Windows XP—Windows Media Player

    - for Windows 7 and higher Windows version—no specific software required

    - for Mac 10.5 or higher OS version—Android File Transfer

2. Create a folder on your computer's hard drive and save the latest software update there by

following the link: https://www.amazon.com/update_Fire_HD10_1 1th_Gen.

3. Connect the charging cable's USB Type-C connector to the appropriate slot on the tablet. Connect the USB Type-A connector to the computer's appropriate slot.

4. Swipe down on the tablet's Home screen and tap on the USB CHARGING button.

5. Hit the Transfer Files option.

6. Open the computer drives folder and double-click the Fire drive to open it.

7. Double-click the folder Internal storage to open it.

8. Drag and drop or copy/cut and paste the software update file into the opened Internal Storage folder.

9. Remove the cable from the tablet's USB Type-C port once the transfer is complete.

10. Swipe down on the tablet's screen and tap on the Gear icon to access Settings or hit the Gear icon on the Home screen. Tap on the Device Options menu.

11.   Hit the System Updates submenu and the UPDATE button, after that.

4.18 How to Disable Safe Mode

1. If your tablet has switched to the Safe Mode accidentally, try to increase and decrease the volume by pressing the Volume up and down. Ensure the button works smoothly and isn't stuck.

2. Press and hold the Power button for several seconds or until the tablet shuts off. If a notification appears on the screen, tap the Power Off option.

3. Wait 3 seconds after pressing the Power button for the tablet to turn on. The Safe Mode is supposed to be displayed.

4.19 How to Remotely Manage Your Stolen or Lost Tablet

Contact Amazon Customer Service to report the loss of the device:

1. Open the Web browser on any available device and go to the Amazon web page for managing content and devices on https://www.amazon.com/mycd.

2. Enter your account information, then hit the CONTINUE button.

3. Click or tap on the tab Devices.

4. Find your tablet model and tap or click on the EDIT button.

5. Under the Serial Number submenu, copy or memorize (write down) the serial number of your tablet.

6. Call Amazon Customer Support at 1-206-922-0880 (for US citizens/residents) or fill out the Customer Support form on https://www.amazon.com/gp/aw/contact-us. Report your tablet as lost or stolen and provide its serial number.

In order to disable purchases from your tablet, follow the instructions for Deregistering Your Tablet.

In order to manage your tablet remotely, the Manage Your Device features must be previously enabled on it. To use the Manage My Device features, follow these steps:

1. Make sure your tablet is connected to the internet via Wi-Fi.

2. Swipe down and tap on the Gear icon to access Settings or hit the Gear icon on the Home screen. Hit the Wireless submenu.

3. Tap on the Location-Based Services option and toggle the switch to the On position. The switch should turn orange.

4. Tap two times on the left-facing arrow on the bottom panel to get back to the Settings menu. Tap on the Device Options submenu.

5. Make sure the switch next to the Find My Tablet option is turned on. The switch should turn orange.

You can control the tablet remotely if the Manage My Device feature is enabled and the tablet is turned on and connected to Wi-Fi. Remotely control your tablet by going to https://www.amazon.com/mycd and performing the following actions:

- Determine the approximate location of the tablet. See where your tablet was last fixed by clicking or tapping on the map on the web page. Within three days, Amazon will send an email to your registered email address informing you of the tablet's status and location.

- Set an alarm. If the tablet is lost, you can set an alarm to prompt the tablet to play the sound for two minutes.

- Deregister the tablet from the Amazon account. This option lets you remove the Amazon account data from the tablet while preserving the personal files (like contacts, photos, etc.) on the tablet. The Amazon apps on the tablet stop working, and purchases are disabled.

- Factory reset the tablet. This operation removes the personal data and files from your tablet, as well as the Amazon account data, and the content previously purchased or downloaded. The latter stays available for other devices registered to your Amazon account, from the Cloud storage.

- Lock the tablet. Works even if your tablet was already set with the lock screen password. You can add a second lock screen password to protect your tablet from unauthorized access.

4.20 How to Close Tabs

1. Tap on the Task Switcher button (the square icon) on the bottom panel on the screen.

2. Choose the app you'd like to close and swipe it to the side.

3. If you'd like to close all opened apps, swipe long to the right side. In the popped-up window, tap on the Close All option.

4.21 How to Use It for Phone

There is no SIM card slot on the tablet. It supports voice and video calls, as well as messaging, through the Alexa app and other apps such as Zoom, Skype, and others.

Making calls via Alexa

1. Make sure your tablet is connected to the internet via Wi-Fi.

2. On the Home screen, tap on the Alexa app.

3. Hit the COMMUNICATE button (the message cloud icon).

4. On the list, locate the contact you want to call and tap on it.

5. Tap the voice call or video call icon to make the call.

6. Hit the END button to end the call.

Another option is to use Alexa's hands-free mode (refer to the "**How to Enable Alexa Hands-Free**" section of the manual) and issue commands such as "Alexa, make a video call to Linda".

Making calls via other messaging apps

1. Make sure your tablet is connected to the internet via Wi-Fi.

2. Tap the Amazon AppStore icon and open the store app.

3. Tap the magnifying glass icon in the top right corner and type in the name of the app you're planning to use.

4. Select the app from the list and tap it. Next to it, tap the DOWNLOAD button.

5. Return to the Home screen by pressing the Home button (the circle icon on the bottom panel).

6. Tap on the messaging app and navigate to its interface to start the communication.

5. Connection

5.1 How to Connect to Wi-Fi on Your Tablet

1. Swipe down and tap on the Wi-Fi icon, or open the Settings menu from the Home page, and tap on the Internet submenu.

2. Switch off the Airplane mode by tapping on the toggle next to it.

3. Enable the Wi-Fi by switching the toggle on next to it.

4. From the list of networks found and presented below, choose the one you want to connect to. Tap on it.

5. Enter the password if required. Tap on the Password field and enter the symbols on the virtual keyboard at the bottom of the screen. Tap on the CONNECT button.

5.2 How to Locate Wi-Fi Password

- Contact your internet provider.

- Lift up your Wi-Fi router carefully and look at the sticker on the bottom. Check if a Wi-Fi password is written there.

- Open the Wi-Fi router's installation manual or the manufacturer's manual. Pay attention to the sections "Access to Wi-Fi", "Connection", etc.

- Check to see if the password can be read from the device already connected to this network. There is a different algorithm for each operating system.

Android

1. Activate the internet browser via the relevant icon on the Home screen.

2. Tap on the web address field and enter the symbols "192.168.1.1". In case the web address of your router is different, it can be found on the bottom sticker of the router.

3. In the pop-up window, enter the "admin" both for login and password. If everything goes well,

the router settings will appear on the screen, including the Wi-Fi password in the applicable area.

4. If the password for administrator access had been changed, open the Wi-Fi menu in the device settings, and tap on the Share option.

5. Make a screenshot of the screen that has a QR-code on it.

6. Launch the QR-Scanner app and scan the screenshot. The Wi-Fi login and password will appear on the display.

MAC OS X

1. Go to the Utilities folder and open it.

2. Activate the Keychain Access application.

3. Click on the network name.

4. Click on the Info menu.

5. Click on the box next to the Show password option.

6. Select the box next to Show password from the drop-down menu.

7. See the Wi-Fi password after entering the administrator password for the MAC device.

Windows PC

(up to Windows 8.1)

1. Log in to the administrator account.

2. Click on the Wireless icon in the bottom taskbar.

3. Locate the network and right-click it.

4. Left-click the Properties option.

5. Left-click the Name or SSID tab to see the network name.

6. Left-click the Security tab to see the network password (next to the Network security key box).

(Windows 8.1 or higher version)

1. Left-click the Wireless icon in the bottom taskbar.

2. Left-click the Network and internet parameters.

3. Left-click the Change adapter settings option.

4. Right-click the icon with the name of the network next to it, and select Status.

5. Left-click the Wireless network properties box.

6. Left-click the Connection tab to see the network name.

7. Left-click the Security tab to see the network password (next to the Network security key box). To view the symbols, you may need to tick the box labeled Show the password.

5.3 What to Do If Your Tablet has Authentication Problems?

1. Make sure the following issues are resolved:

   - Check the status of other devices connected to the same network. Make sure that the internet connection is stable and isn't limited. If the status is Disconnected or you can't access the websites through the device, for a solution, contact your internet provider.

   - Swipe down on the tablet screen and tap on the Wireless icon. Check the status of the Airplane mode. If it's on, tap on it once to inactivate the icon and set the Airplane mode to Off.

   - Make sure the Wi-Fi password is filled in correctly. Pay attention to the symbols, digits, capital letters. If you can't find the Wi-fi password, address the **"How to Locate Wi-Fi Password"** section.

   - Check if the tablet software is updated to the latest version available. Upgrade to the latest software version by connecting to another available network or downloading it to a USB flash drive and installing it on your tablet.

2. Switch the Wi-Fi toggle off, then return it to the on position.

3. Press and hold the Power button. Wait for 40 seconds or until the tablet restarts. Release the button after the restart or if 40 seconds have passed. If the tablet turns off but doesn't restart after 40 seconds, press the Power button again to start the tablet.

4. Swipe down and tap on the Wireless icon, then on Wi-Fi. Check if the name of your preferred network is included in the list. If it doesn't, tap the SCAN button. If the network doesn't appear on the list, move closer to the Wi-Fi router and press the SCAN button again.

5. Make sure the Wi-Fi router is set on Wi-Fi channels from 1 to 11. If not, go to your router's settings and adjust the channels as needed. Consult the router manufacturer's guide or the internet provide service, for assistance.

6. Disconnect your Wi-Fi router and modem from the power source. Wait for 30 seconds. Plug in the modem adapter back into the network. When the modem is turned on (in most models, the LED indicators will light up),

plug the Wi-Fi router into the outlet. Make sure that the router is activated (for example, check if another device can connect to the Wi-Fi network). Repeat the steps to connect your tablet to the network.

5.4 What to Do If You Have Troubles Connecting Your Tablet

In order to restart the Wi-Fi connection, power cycle your modem and Wi-Fi router.

1. Disconnect the modem (a box that ensures the connection to the WAN) from the electric outlet.

2. Unplug the router (the box with antennas that distributes the signal from the modem to the LAN devices) from the outlet.

3. Allow a few minutes to pass.

4. Plug in the modem adapter into the outlet. Wait until the LED indicators' flashing pattern settles into a regular pattern.

5. Connect the Wi-Fi router to power. Wait for a minute.

6. Connect other devices to Wi-Fi and make sure the signal and the internet access are sufficient.

7. Reconnect your tablet to Wi-Fi.

5.5 How to Customize Bluetooth Keyboard Shortcuts

1. Swipe down and tap on the Gear icon on the opened panel or open Settings from the Home screen. Tap on the Device options menu, and then on the System Updates submenu. Tap on the UPDATE button, if available. The tablet should restart, and the notification Installing system updates should appear on display.

2. Swipe down and tap on the Gear icon or open Settings from the Home screen. Tap on the Device options menu.

3. Tap on the Keyboard & Language submenu.

4. Tap on the Physical Keyboard option.

5. Tap on the option Email Shortcut Key or Files Shortcut Key.

6. Choose the app from the list and tap on its name to assign it to the key.

5.6 Is It Possible to Connect the Tablet to the Internet via a Wire?

Wi-Fi is the only way to connect to the internet. If you have a wired internet connection to your PC or another device, check if you can share Wi-Fi with your tablet from that device.

5.7 How to Plug Your Tablet into a Car

1. Connect the charging cable's USB Type-C connector to the appropriate slot on the tablet.

2. Insert the USB Type-A connector of the cable into the relevant slot on your car's head unit. If there's no USB port, you can plug the connector into the USB cigarette lighter device.

6. Registration

6.1 How to Register Device on Your Amazon Account

1. Make sure the time zone and time displayed on the tablet match your local time zone and time.

2. Make sure that your tablet software is upgraded to the latest version. Otherwise, swipe down and tap on the Gear icon or open Settings straight from the Home screen. Tap on the Device options menu and then on the System Updates submenu. Tap on Update. The tablet should restart, and the notification Installing system updates should appear on display.

3. Check if the Wi-Fi connection is working properly.

4. Swipe down and tap on the Gear icon or open Settings straight from the Home screen.

5. Tap on the Register option.

6. Enter the email linked to your Amazon account and then the password into the corresponding fields. Tap the CONTINUE button.

7. Double-check that your Amazon account's login and password are correct. If you forgot the password, tap on the Forgot the password option and change your password. Then, log in again. In case you don't have an Amazon account yet, tap on the START HERE button under the inscription "New to Amazon?", and create a new account.

6.2 How to Fix Possible Registration Issues

Before registering your tablet or app, there are a few things you should do first:

- Make sure that your tablet software is upgraded to the latest version. Otherwise, swipe down and tap on the Gear icon or open Settings straight from the Home screen. Tap on the Device options menu and then on the System Updates submenu. Tap on Update. The tablet should restart, and the notification Installing system updates should appear on display.

- The email and mobile number you are entering to register are the same that have been used to log into your Amazon account.

- Check your email client's Junk or Spam folders for registration emails before logging in. Disable the filters of the email client in order to see all the incoming emails.

In case additional registration steps are required:

1. Confirm that you'll be registering your tablet or app. Check the relevant box or tap on the Confirm/Register button.

2. In the Login field, enter the email or a phone number assigned to your current Amazon account. Depending on the type of data you inserted in the Login field, the text will be sent to your email address or to your mobile phone.

3. Launch your email client or check your smartphone for incoming messages. There should be a one-time password. The password is usually valid for 10 minutes after it is received.

4. Enter the one-time password into the Password field in the app you want to register.

6.3 How to Pass a Two-Step Verification

If a message appears during registration, asking you to enter a security code, it means that you have to pass the Two-Step Verification process. For some apps that do not request the unique security code, the registration process might end up in an error even if the correct login and password are used.

In this case, the Two-Step Verification sign-in is required.

1. Fill in your email or mobile number in the Login field, and your password in the Password field. Below, tap on the SUBMIT button.

2. If a Two-Step Verification is activated, an error message appears on display indicating the login and password are incorrect.

3. A security code is sent to your smartphone or email as a text message, a voice call, or through the app authenticator.

4. Copy or memorize the security code and fill it in the Password field right after your usual password code, without spaces or other symbols.

If you forgot your account password, you can use the one-time password to register for an app.

1. In the Login field, type your email address or a phone number, then tap on the SUBMIT button.

2. Open your email client or check your smartphone for incoming messages. There should be a one-time password. The password is usually valid for 10 minutes after it is received.

3. In the app, you need to register to enter the one-time password in the appropriate field.

4. A security code is sent to your smartphone or email as a text message, a voice call, or through the app authenticator.

5. Copy or memorize the security code, then enter it in the Password field after your regular password, without spaces or other extra symbols.

6.4 How to Change Your Device Name

1. Make sure your tablet is connected to Wi-Fi.

2. Run the internet browser via the browser icon on the Home screen.

3. Proceed to the Manage Your Content and Devices page.

4. Enter your account information, then tap on the CONTINUE button.

5. Tap on the Devices tab.

6. Tap on the name of your tablet on the list.

7. Tap on the Edit option next to the current tablet name.

8. Enter the new name, and tap on the SAVE button.

6.5 How to Deregister Your Tablet

1. Make sure your tablet is connected to the internet via Wi-Fi.

2. Launch the internet browser via taping the relevant icon on the Home screen.

3. Proceed to the Manage Your Content and Devices page.

4. Enter your account information, then tap on the CONTINUE button.

5. Tap on the Devices tab.

6. Tap on the name of your tablet on the list.

7. Tap on the option Deregister and confirm the operation.

7. Charging

7.1 How to Wirelessly Charge the Device

In order to charge your tablet, use Qi-certified devices (docks and mats) and "Made for Amazon" gadgets. Visit the following page to learn more about compatible charging devices: https://www.amazon.com/b?node=23448661011.

1. Connect the dock station to the outlet if required. If it's powered from the internal battery, turn the dock station on.

2. Place the tablet in the dock station's center, either vertically or horizontally. Make sure its position is stable.

3. If the charging has started, the LED indicator on the dock station turns solid white.

4. When the charging is finished, the LED indicator turns off. You can take the tablet out and use it.

7.2 How to Fix Possible Wireless Charging Issues

- Ensure the wireless dock station is Qi-certified. Some of the models can still be incompatible with your tablet. For more information, visit the page: https://www.amazon.com/b?node=2344866101 1.

- Make sure the tablet is placed firmly on the dock station or a wireless charging mat. The center of the tablet should be in the center of the charging surface of the dock station.

- Make sure the dock station is connected to an outlet or has enough internal battery charge.

- Try using it to charge another device and see if it works.

- If the tablet is wrapped in a cover, remove it.

- Press the Power button for 40 seconds or until the tablet shuts off. Press and hold the Power button until the screen lights up if the tablet does not restart automatically.

7.3 How to Solve a Liquid-Detection Alert

If a blue picture with three water drops and the alert sign above appears on the screen of your tablet, the liquid is detected within the USB-C port. The alert audio signal appears alongside the pop-up icon.

1. If the tablet is charging when the Liquid Alert appears, disconnect the USB-C cable from the outlet and unplug it from the tablet as soon as possible. The audio and visual alerts cannot be disabled until the charging cable is disconnected from the USB-C port of the tablet.

2. With the USB-C port facing down, hold the tablet vertically. Shake it gently for about 5 seconds.

3. Inspect the USB-C port to check if there's visible liquid present. If positive, repeat step 2.

4. Place the tablet on the flat horizontal surface in the dry environment until the visual and audio alerts disappear. In some cases, drying can take up to 48 hours.

5. While the liquid is detected, the tablet can be used for various operations except for charging. Charging is prohibited until the visual and audio alerts completely disappear. After that, you may need to reset the tablet. Press and hold the Power button for 40 seconds or until the tablet shuts off. If the tablet doesn't restart automatically, press and hold the Power button until the screen lights up.

8. Apps

8.1 How to Install an App on Your Device

For apps you've saved in your library, go to:

1. Swipe to the left to get to the Library screen.

2. Tap on the Downloaded tab.

3. Choose an app you want to download and tap on it.

4. After the app is downloaded, tap on the orange OPEN button to launch it.

For new apps you are going to install:

1. On the Home screen, find the Amazon Appstore menu and tap on it.

2. Start inserting the app's name in the field on the top. The available apps with similar names will appear on the screen.

3. Select the app from the list and tap the DOWNLOAD button.

4. When the app is downloaded, tap on the orange OPEN button to launch it.

8.2 How to Fix Possible App Errors

1. Close the app. At the bottom of the screen, press the square icon. To find the app you want to close, swipe up or down. Swipe the app miniature to the side or tap the Cross symbol at the top of the miniature when it appears in the middle of the screen.

2. Restart the tablet. Hold down the Power button for 40 seconds. After the tablet restarts, launch the app again to see if the issue has been resolved.

3. Uninstall the app and install it back. Select the Apps & notifications menu in Settings, select All, and find the app you need. Tap on it and open its settings. Hit the button UNINSTALL. After the app is deleted, return to the Home screen. Swipe down to the left and open the library. Hit the tab Downloaded, find the app, and tap to install it.

8.3 How to Force Close an App

1. Swipe down, and tap on the Gear icon to access the settings. Select the Apps & notifications section.

2. Press the downward-facing arrow on the right side of the top bar. From the dropdown menu, select Running apps.

3. On the list, locate the app you want to close and tap it.

4. At the top of the screen, hit the button FORCE CLOSE.

8.4 How to Clear an App's Data and Cache

1. To access Settings, swipe down and tap the Gear icon. Select the Apps & Notifications option from the drop-down menu.

2. Tap on the Manage ALL APPLICATIONS button.

3. Locate the app you require on the list beneath the button and tap it to access its settings.

4. Hit the button STORAGE, then, tap on the CLEAR STORAGE button.

5. Tap the CLEAR CACHE button.

8.5 How to Move Apps on Screen

1. Find the app icon on the screen.

2. Hold your finger on the app icon.

3. Drag your finger to the location where you want the app to be moved.

4. Pull your finger away from the screen. If you "drop" an app over another app icon, a folder containing both apps will be created.

8.6 How to Install Google Play Store

There's no official way to install the Google Play Store app on your tablet. The options below include downloading the software content from external websites. Pay attention to the manufacturer and source of the software content. If you have any doubts about the software's or source's authenticity or safety, do not proceed with the installation.

How to install the Google Play Store directly:

1. Make sure your tablet system update is the latest available. Refer to the section of the manual titled **"How to Install the Software Updates"**.

2. Remove the SD card from your tablet in order to prevent Google Play Store from being installed onto it.

3. Hold down the Power button on the right side of the tablet for 3 seconds or until the tablet turns off.

4. If the notification message appears on the screen, tap on the Power Off option.

5. Open the SD card cover and press lightly on the inserted SD card. Remove the popped-out SD card and close the cover.

6. Swipe down and tap on the Gear icon to access Settings or tap the Gear icon on the Home screen. Hit the Security & Privacy submenu.

7. Tap on Apps from Unknown Sources option.

8. Tap the Silk Browser icon, the "Allow from this source" inscription appears below. Tap on the switch next to it in order to enable the function. The switch should change to orange.

9. Hit the Home button (the circle icon) on the bottom panel to get to the Home screen. Tap the Silk browser app to run the browser.

10.   Download the following APK files by entering the web links into the browser address field (on top of the window):

- Google Play Store—from the source https://www.apkmirror.com/apk/google-inc/google-play-store/google-play-store-21-6-13-release/google-play-store-21-6-13-21-0-pr-327913455-android-apk-download/

- Google Play Services—from the source https://www.apkmirror.com/apk/google-inc/google-play-services/google-play-services-20-30-65-release/google-play-services-20-30-65-100400-328153085-android-apk-download/

- Google Account Manager—from the source https://www.apkmirror.com/apk/google-inc/google-account-manager/google-account-manager-7-1-2-release/google-account-manager-7-1-2-android-apk-download/

- Google Services Framework—from the source https://www.apkmirror.com/apk/google-inc/google-services-framework/google-services-framework-9-4832352-release/google-services-framework-9-4832352-android-apk-download/

Follow one of the links above, hit the DOWNLOAD APK button, and then tap OK.

11. Hit the Home button (the circle icon) on the bottom panel to get to the Home screen. Tap the Files app to view the files you downloaded.

12. Hit the Google Account Manager file. The warning notification window will appear. Tap CONTINUE to install the app. If a notification with an offer to install the update appears, hit INSTALL at the bottom of the screen, and proceed to the next file. Install files in the following order:

- Google Account Manager

- Google Services Framework

- Google Play Services

- Google Play Store

13.   After all the apps are successfully installed, restart the tablet. Hold down the Power button for 40 seconds or until the tablet restarts.

14.   On the Home screen, tap on the Google Play Store app. Enter your Google account information under the "Sign In" inscription or create a Google account by tapping the Create account option. Tap Next to proceed.

How to install the Google Play Store on a Windows computer:

1. To prevent the Google Play Store from being installed on your tablet, remove the SD card.

2. Hold down the Power button on the right side of the tablet for three seconds or until it turns off.

3. Tap the Power Off option if the notification message appears on the screen.

4. Open the SD card cover and press lightly on the inserted SD card. Remove the popped-out SD card and close the cover.

5. Swipe down and tap on the Gear icon to access Settings or hit the Gear icon on the Home screen. Hit the Device Options submenu.

6. Tap the Serial Number digits several times (up to ten times) to disclose the Developer Options menu.

7. Tap on the Developer Options and find the Debugging submenu. Under this submenu, hit the switch next to the Enable ADB option. The switch should change to orange.

8. If your computer's OS is Windows 10 or Windows 8, you'll need to disable driver signature enforcement on your computer:

   • for Windows 8, open the PC settings, proceed to the More PC Settings, and then go to the General menu

   • for Windows 10, open the PC settings, proceed to the Update and Security menu, then to the Recovery submenu

The following steps are the same for Windows 8 and Windows 10:

   • Find the Advanced Startup option and left-click the RESTART NOW button. The screen with the reboot options appears.

- Left-click the Troubleshoot menu and proceed to the Advanced Options submenu, then to the Startup settings options.

- Left-click Disable driver signature enforcement and left-click the RESTART button.

Note: If your PC restarts after the reboot restart, you'll have to repeat the disabling procedure.

9. Close all opened apps. Hit the Task Switcher button (the square icon on the bottom of the screen), and swipe to the side all opened apps to close them.

10.   If your computer's OS is Windows 10, the necessary drivers are already installed and ready to use as soon as your tablet is connected. For earlier Windows OS versions, you might need to install the Google USB Driver onto your tablet. Perform the following steps:

1. Tap on the Silk Browser icon on the Home screen to launch the app.

2. Copy and paste the following web address into the relevant field of the browser (on top): https://developer.android.com/studio/run/win -usb

3. Tap on the DOWNLOAD button. A notification will appear at the bottom of the screen. Tap on the Open option.

4. Find the installation file within the ZIP folder opened, and tap on it. Hit the INSTALL button to complete the installation.

5. Connect the charging cable's USB Type-C connector to the appropriate slot on the tablet. Connect the USB Type-A connector to the computer's (with Windows 8 and higher OS version) appropriate slot.

6. In the popped window, tap CONFIRM to enable the debugging mode.

7. Check the computer's Drives folder to see if the tablet is listed under the My PC menu.

8. Download the software tool to your PC from https://rootjunkysdl.com/?dir=Amazon%20Fir e%205th%20gen/SuperTool. Unzip the files. Find the first .bat file and left-click it to run it. The window titled "Amazon Fire Tablet Tool" should appear on your PC desktop.

9. Press the 1 key and then Enter. Another window must appear, with an installation option for the ADB driver.

10. Press the 1 key and then Enter. The window with the system requirements appears.

11. Press any key on your PC keyboard. The Windows Device Manager window should open.

12. Left-click the tab Universal Serial Bus device and locate your tablet on the list.

13. Right-click the tablet, then left-click the UPDATE DRIVER SOFTWARE button.

14. Left-click the option Browse my computer for driver software, then left-click Let me pick from the list of devices..., then left-click on the Have Disk option.

15. Within the browsing window, left-click the USB_drivers folder that was downloaded along with the software tool.

16. Locate the "android_winusb.inf" file, left-click to open it. Left-click the OK button.

17. On the bottom panel on your PC screen, left-click the Super Tool tab, and open the appropriate window.

18. Press any key on our PC keyboard, and then Enter key in order to return to the main menu of the software tool.

19. Activate the "first .bat" file in the software, and press 2 to install the Google Play files. Press any key on your keyboard. The software should prompt the four stages of installation, upon which the Google Play Store app should appear on your tablet Home screen.

Tip: The Google Play Store isn't supported by the tablet by default. Installing the Google Play Store, you will get a tablet-oriented version of the Google Play Store. Installation of the Google Play Store doesn't affect your tablet speed and performance.

8.7 How to Install YouTube App

There's no official way to install the YouTube app on your tablet. The options below include downloading the software content from external websites. Pay attention to the manufacturer and source of the software content. If you have any doubts about the software's or source's authenticity or safety, do not proceed with the installation.

Sideload the YouTube app

1. Make sure your tablet's operating system update is the latest available. Refer to the section of the manual titled **"How to Install the Software Updates"**.

2. To prevent the Google Play Store from being installed on your tablet, remove the SD card.

3. Hold down the Power button at the right-hand side for 3 seconds or until the tablet turns off.

4. If the notification message appears on the screen, tap on the Power Off option.

5. Open the SD card cover and press lightly on the inserted SD card. Remove the popped-out SD card and close the cover.

6. Swipe down and tap on the Gear icon to access Settings or hit the Gear icon on the Home screen. Hit the Security & Privacy submenu.

7. Tap on Apps from Unknown Sources option.

8. Tap the Silk Browser icon, the "Allow from this source" inscription appears below. Tap the switch next to it in order to enable the function. The switch should change orange.

9. Restart the tablet. Hold down the Power button for 40 seconds or until it restarts.

10. Download the file with the APK extension for the YouTube app. There are two ways to do that.

Via Silk Browser:

1. Hit the Home button (the circle icon) on the bottom panel to get to the Home screen. Tap the Silk browser app to launch the browser.

2. Tap on the web address field on top and enter the website address apkmirror.com. To visit the website, simply tap.

3. Locate the YouTube app on the list corresponding to the latest Android version, and tap on it. Hit the DOWNLOAD APK button.

4. In the warning window, click OK to start downloading the file.

5. After the installation is complete, the notification appears at the bottom of the screen. Tap it to open the file.

6. Scroll down to the bottom and select INSTALL.

Via the Android-driven smartphone:

1. Download and install the APK Extractor app on your Android smartphone.

2. Open the APK Extractor app and find the YouTube file on the list.

3. Tap on the three dots button next to the file. A window will pop offering the actions to be performed with the file.

4. Tap on the Share option and select the appropriate way of sharing. As the APK files are usually large, the best option would be to save the file to OneDrive or Dropbox.

5. On your tablet, access the OneDrive or Dropbox and tap on the DOWNLOAD button.

6. Hit the INSTALL button at the bottom of the screen. The YouTube app icon should appear on your tablet's Home screen.

Download the YouTube app from the PC

1. Make sure your tablet system update is the latest available. Refer to the section of the manual titled **"How to Install the Software Updates"**.

2. Remove the SD card from your tablet in order to prevent the Google Play Store from being installed onto it.

3. Hold down the Power button at the right-hand side for 3 seconds or until the tablet turns off.

4. If the notification message appears on the screen, tap on the Power Off option.

5. Open the SD card cover and press lightly on the inserted SD card. Remove the popped-out SD card and close the cover.

6. Swipe down and tap on the Gear icon to access Settings or hit the Gear icon on the Home screen. Hit the Security & Privacy submenu.

7. Tap on Apps from Unknown Sources option.

8. Tap the Silk Browser icon, the "Allow from this source" inscription appears below. Tap the switch next to it in order to enable the function. The switch should change to orange.

9. Restart the tablet. Hold down the Power button for 40 seconds or until it restarts.

10. On your PC, open the web browser and download the YouTube APK file from the website apkmirror.com.

11. Connect the charging cable's USB Type-C connector to the appropriate slot on the tablet. Connect the USB Type-A connector to the computer's appropriate slot.

12. Check the computer's Drives folder to see if the tablet is listed under the My PC menu.

13. Open the Download folder by left-clicking the tablet drive in the PC panel.

14. Copy and paste the YouTube APK file into the Download folder.

15. On your tablet's Home screen, tap the Amazon Appstore app, and find the ES File Explorer app.

16. Tap to install the app on your tablet and hit the OPEN button after the installation is complete.

17. Locate the Download folder and tap on it to open.

18.   Tap the YouTube icon and hit the INSTALL button at the bottom to install the app. The YouTube app is supposed to appear on your tablet's Home screen.

*Tip: Due to the absence of the Google Play Store app, the YouTube app may not run or may stop running at any time. In order to install the Google Play Store app, refer to the "**How to Install Google Play Store**" section of the manual.*

8.8 How to Install Microsoft Office on Your Tablet

Download the Microsoft Office mobile app from Amazon Appstore

Microsoft Word, Microsoft Excel, and Microsoft PowerPoint are all included in the Microsoft Office Mobile app for Amazon. This app comes with the following features:

- create word documents, excel sheets, and presentations

- edit documents and presentations

- sign documents with one tap

- make quick notes

- convert files into the PDF format

- extract text from a picture/PDF into a Word document or Excel table

In order to download the Microsoft Office app from the Amazon Appstore, take the following steps:

1. On the Home screen, tap the Amazon Appstore icon.

2. Tap the magnifying glass icon in the top right corner of the screen and type the "Microsoft Office" on the virtual keyboard that appears at the bottom of the screen. Otherwise, tap the Home tab and scroll down to find the Microsoft Office app on the list.

3. Locate the Microsoft Office Mobile app and hit the GET button next to it.

4. The billing notification will be sent to your email. Tap to confirm the purchase.

5. Tap on the Home button (the circle icon on the bottom panel) to return to the Home screen.

6. Scroll down your Home screen and find the Microsoft Office icon or tap the Apps icon and search the list for the Microsoft Office Mobile app.

Download the Microsoft Office tools from the Google Play Store

The Google Play Store allows you to install the Microsoft Office tools as standalone apps.

1. Refer to the "**How to Install Google Play Store**" section of the manual to install the Google Play Store on your tablet.

2. On the Home screen, tap on the Google Play Store icon.

3. Enter your Google account information under the "Sign In" inscription or create a Google account by tapping on Create account option. Tap Next to proceed.

4. Tap on the top bar with the magnifying glass icon on the left. Enter the name of the Microsoft Office app you want to install.

5. Tap on the app on the dropdown list below.

6. Hit the INSTALL button below.

7. Tap on the Home button (the circle icon on the bottom panel) to return to the Home screen.

8. Scroll down your Home screen and locate the Microsoft Office tool icon.

8.9 How to Install a Map Program for Cars

The tablet doesn't have a built-in GPS module, but it does support location-based services via Wi-Fi.

1. Make sure your tablet is connected to the internet via Wi-Fi.

2. Swipe down and tap on the Gear icon to access Settings or hit the Gear icon on the Home screen. Hit the Wireless submenu.

3. Tap on the Location-Based Services option and toggle the switch to the On position. The switch should change to orange.

4. Hit the Home button (the circle icon on the bottom panel) and return to the Home screen.

5. Tap on the Amazon Appstore icon to open it.

6. Tap the magnifying glass icon in the top right corner and type in the "Maps" word.

7. Find the suitable maps and tap on the app. Tap the DOWNLOAD button.

8. Hit the Home button (the circle icon on the bottom panel) and return to the Home screen.

9. Swipe to the left to get on the Library screen.

10.   Tap on the maps app and hit the INSTALL button.

11.   Hit the Home button (the circle icon on the bottom panel) and return to the Home screen. Scroll down to find the installed maps app.

8.10 Can a Preloaded App be Deleted?

Some of the pre-installed apps (Settings, Alexa, Kindle, etc.) on your tablet cannot be deleted. Yet, there are also the ones you can remove permanently (the ones you download by yourself).

1. Swipe down and tap on the Gear icon to access Settings or hit the Gear icon on the Home screen. Hit the Apps & Games submenu.

2. Hit the Manage All Applications option. A list of all the apps installed on the tablet will appear.

3. Scroll down and find the app you'd like to delete, tap on it.

4. Hit the UNINSTALL button on the right.

5. Tap the OK button in the popped-up notification window.

8.11 How to Download the Hoopla App

The Hoopla app is available in the Amazon Appstore.

1. Make sure your tablet is connected to the internet via Wi-Fi.

2. Tap the Amazon Appstore icon and launch the store app.

3. Tap the magnifying glass icon in the top right corner and type in the "Hoopla" word.

4. Find the app and tap on it. Hit the DOWNLOAD button next to it.

5. Hit the Home button (the circle icon on the bottom panel) and return to the Home screen. Scroll down to find the installed Hoopla app.

8.12 How to Install Games on the Tablet

1. Make sure your tablet is connected to the internet via Wi-Fi.

2. Tap the Amazon Appstore icon and run the store app.

3. Tap the magnifying glass icon in the top right corner and type in the name of the game you'd like to install.

4. Locate the game on and tap on it. Hit the DOWNLOAD button next to it.

5. Hit the Home button (the circle icon on the bottom panel) and return to the Home screen.

6. Tap the Games app and find the installed game.

9. Game Mode

9.1 How to Enable Game Mode

1. To access Settings, swipe down and tap the Gear icon. Select the Apps & Notifications option.

2. Find the Game mode option and tap on the toggle next to it to set it to the On position (the option turns orange).

Tip: When you activate Game mode, you will be able to ignore notifications from other apps (messaging, email, Alexa, and so on) while playing a game. If a game app is open, the notifications will not appear on the screen.

9.2 How to Disable Game Mode

1. Swipe down and tap on the Gear icon to access Settings. Select the Apps & Notifications option.

2. Switch the Game mode option to the Off position by tapping on the toggle next to it (the switch should turn blue).

10. Print

10.1 How to Print Copies from Your Tablet

1. Power on the printer and connect it to the same Wi-Fi network that your tablet is connected to.

2. Open the web page or a document you want to print, on your tablet.

3. Tap on three vertical dots in the top right corner and hit the Print option.

4. In the top left corner, the name of the connected printer will appear. If the selected printer isn't available, tap on the name and select another printer from the dropdown menu.

5. Below the printer's name, tap on the line "Copies" in order to change the number of copies for printing or amend other settings. Additional options can be accessed by pressing the MORE OPTIONS button.

6. Tap the orange printer icon to start to print.

10.2 How to Add a Printer Manually

1. Make sure that your printer is compatible with the tablet. For that, visit mopria.org and enter your printer manufacturer and/or model, then press Search. If your printer model is listed, you can use it with the tablet.

2. Tap on three vertical dots in the top right corner and hit the Print option.

3. The name of the connected printer will show in the upper left corner. Select another printer from the selection list by tapping on the name. Unfold the list by tapping the ALL PRINTERS button.

4. Tap on the Plus icon to add a printer manually.

5. Enter the IP address of your printer and tap to confirm.

11. Kindle

11.1 How to Download Books from Amazon Library

1. To access the Library, swipe left from the Home screen. If not, open the Kindle app and select the Library option.

2. Hit the ALL button on the left side of the screen. Below is a complete list of Amazon goods that have been previously purchased and downloaded.

3. Choose any book and tap on it to download it.

12. Battery

12.1 How to Conserve Battery Power

To access Settings, swipe down and tap the Gear icon, or press the Gear icon on the Home screen.

- Tap on the Display option and select the Brightness level button. Then tap on the circle on the slider on the top and drag it to the left to dim the screen.

- Tap on the Display option and select the Sleep menu. Tap on the circle next to the "15 seconds" option to decrease the screen timeout time (the circle next to the selected option turns orange).

- Tap on the Device options menu and select the System updates submenu. Disable the UPDATE button by tapping on it and turning it grey.

- Tap on the Battery option and tap on the switch next to the Automatic Smart Suspend line (the switch turns orange). The Automatic Smart Suspend helps save the battery charge by disabling and enabling the Wi-Fi connection.

- To turn the volume down and spend less battery charge for powering the speakers, press the lower part of the volume button on the right side of the tablet.

12.2 What is Smart Suspend?

Smart Suspend allows you to manage your internet connection in order to save battery life and reduce traffic usage. The automatic smart suspend feature allows your tablet to analyze how you use it and turn on or off the internet connection when you're most likely to need it or not.

How to manage the Smart Suspend manually:

1. Swipe down and tap on the Gear icon to access Settings or hit the Gear icon on the Home screen.

2. Tap on the Battery option and tap on the switch next to the Automatic Smart Suspend line. The switch turns grey.

3. Tap on the Scheduled Smart Suspend option.

4. Set the desired start and end times for the internet connection.

12.3 How to Turn On Battery Saver

1. Swipe down and tap on the Gear icon to access Settings or hit the Gear icon on the Home screen. Tap on the Battery option.

2. Activate the saving mode or set the automatic battery saving mode:

   - Tap on the switch next to the Low Power Mode to activate the power-consuming mode (the switch turns orange).

   - Tap on the Automatic Low Power Mode submenu. Tap on and drag the circle on the slider in order to establish the battery level, at which the battery saving mode will be activated.

13. Household Profiles

13.1 How to Create a Child Profile

1. Swipe down and tap on the Gear icon to access Settings or hit the Gear icon on the Home screen. Tap on the Profiles & family Library option.

2. Hit the submenu Add a child profile.

3. On the right, tap the Set password option.

4. Fill in the child's name, age, and gender in the profile.

5. Hit the ADD PROFILE button.

13.2 How to Add Profile to Your Household

1. Swipe down and tap on the Gear icon to access Settings or hit the Gear icon on the Home screen. Tap on the Profiles & family Library option.

2. Tap on the Add adult submenu. Hit the CONTINUE button in the window that has appeared.

3. Choose whether you want to use an existing Amazon account or create a new one. Tap on the circle to the right of the suitable option to select it (the circle turns orange). Hit the CONTINUE button below.

4. Enter your household's Amazon account information or create a new Amazon account, then click the CONTINUE button.

5. Choose whether the additional account will be able to share payment methods, content, and the Prime membership, or whether it will be limited to its own content and management of the child profiles. Tap on the relevant circle on the right to select this option (the circle turns orange). Hit the CONTINUE button.

14. Parental Control

14.1 What is Parental Control?

You may use the following settings to manage Parental Control on your tablet:

- Set the child's daily time to use your tablet.

- Limit access to the content of certain types (e.g. downloaded or camera shots, games, books, etc.).

- Limit access to tablet functions.

What features can be restricted:

- Making payments/reading the data of a credit card linked to the Amazon account

- Browsing the internet

- Using the camera

- Watching Prime videos' previews

- Wi-Fi and Bluetooth access

- Accessing and managing Contacts

- Accessing and managing Email client

- Accessing and managing Calendar

- Using location-tracking services

How to manage access to content and features on your tablet:

- Create a child's profile and enable or disable access to certain applications or content for that account.

- Swipe down and tap on the Gear icon to access Settings or hit the Gear icon on the Home screen. Tap on the Parental Controls menu. Hit the Amazon Content and Apps submenu, and tap on the button next to each type of content and category you want to limit access to. The button should be set to BLOCKED if you want to restrict access to the corresponding content.

14.2 How to Enable Parental Control

1. Swipe down and tap on the Gear icon to access Settings or hit the Gear icon on the Home screen. Tap on the Parental Controls menu.

2. Toggle the toggle switch to the On position by tapping it (the switch becomes orange).

3. Enter the password for your parental control in the dropdown window, and then enter it again in the field below. To see the passwords you've entered, tap the square next to the "Hide password" inscription and edit them to match each other if needed.

4. Tap on the FINISH button below. At the top of the screen, the lock icon will appear signalizing the parental control mode is activated. The web browser, camera, contacts, calendar, email client, Alexa, and videos will be blocked by default.

14.3 How to Control Content on a Child Profile

1. Download the apps and content you'd like to add to your child's profile, to your tablet, computer, or laptop.

2. To access the Parent Dashboard, go to https://parents.amazon.com/ via your tablet's, computer's, or laptop's browser.

3. Fill out the form with your Amazon account information and tap/left-click the SIGN-IN button below.

4. Choose your child's profile from the list of icons and tap/left-click the GET STARTED button below. The profile information will appear on the screen.

5. Tap/left-click the Gear icon next to the profile's name and access the Settings menu for that profile.

6. Tap/left-click the Add content option. A list of contents will appear on the screen.

7. Select the tab corresponding to the content category you'd like to add (e.g. Apps, Audible, etc.).

8. Find the content you'd like to add (on the list) and tap/click on the toggle switch next to it. The switch should turn orange.

Content that cannot be added to the profile:

- Music/audio records

- Personal files

- Prime videos

- Rentals for Prime video

14.4 How to Adjust Communication Features

You can restrict or allow the following operations for your child by managing the communication features:

- Outbound voice and video calls to the devices with Alexa enabled. These devices can be a part of your household Alexa system or not belong to it.

- Make outbound calls to all or selected contacts.

- Managing the Alexa-enabled devices that are part of your home's Alexa system.

How to manage the communication features:

1. Access the Parent Dashboard on https://parents.amazon.com/ through the browser of your computer, tablet, or laptop.

2. Fill out the form below with your Amazon account information and tap/left-click the SIGN-IN button.

3. Choose your child's profile from the list of icons and tap/left-click the GET STARTED button

below. The profile information will appear on the screen.

4. To access the profile's settings menu, tap on/left-click the Gear icon next to the profile's name.

5. Scroll down to the menu Fire Tablet Settings. Tap/left-click the Manage Communications submenu below it.

6. Tap/left-click the GRANT PARENTAL CONSENT button if you want to give your child access to certain features (with the exclamation sign icon on the left). Tap/left-click the HIDE THESE FEATURES ON THE FIRE TABLET button if you want to limit your child's access to certain features.

7. To enable or disable the features for your child, tap/left-click the toggle switches next to each feature (Announcements and Calling).

14.5 How to Approve Contact for Your Child

1. Tap the Alexa app icon on the Home screen to open the app.

2. Tap on the Communicate icon at the bottom of the app window.

3. Hit the Contacts icon in the top right corner of the screen.

4. Tap the toggle switch to the On position (the switch should turn orange).

5. To access the profile contact options, first hit your name, then your child's profile name.

6. Tap on the Add New Contact option. Fill out the contact information or choose a contact from the dropdown list.

14.6 How to Approve Purchases from Your Child's Account

1. When you receive an email notification regarding a download or purchase request, press the link to the Parents Dashboard, or go to https://parents.amazon.com/.

2. To approve or reject a request, choose the tick next to it. Approve or reject the request by left clicking/ tapping the appropriate option.

3. A notification of the approval or rejection of the request is sent to the Quick Settings panel of your tablet. The child must tap on the notification to open the download page.

15. Data Storage

15.1 How to Run MicroSD on Your Tablet

1. Make sure the tablet's battery is fully charged. Charge it if needed (refer to the "Charge the Battery" section of the manual).

2. Check if the software versions are up to date. Install the updates manually if necessary (Refer to the **"How to Install Software Updates"** section of the manual).

3. Turn off your tablet by holding the Power button for 20 seconds or until it shuts off. If a notification window appears on the screen, tap on the Power Off button.

4. Open the SD card cover and press lightly on the inserted SD card. Remove the popped-out SD card and close the cover.

5. Wait for 60 seconds, then insert the microSD card back into its compartment. Close the rubber cover.

6. Press and hold the Power button for 3 seconds or until the tablet turns on.

7. Ascertain that your tablet is registered to your Amazon account. Open the Silk browser ad tap on the top bar to enter the web address for the Manage Your Content and Devices web page. Enter your account information, then tap on the CONTINUE button. Tap on the Devices tab and find your tablet among the listed gadgets.

8. Swipe down and tap on the Gear icon to access Settings or hit the Gear icon on the Home screen. Hit the Storage submenu. Tap on the SD Card option. Hit the switches next to the listed content categories shifting their positions. All switches are supposed to be in the On positions (colored orange).

9. Format the microSD card. Refer to the "**How to Delete All Data from Your SD Card**" section of the manual.

10.   Format the microSD card via the PC or laptop:

   • Turn off your tablet by holding the Power button for 20 seconds or until it shuts off. If a notification window appears on the screen, tap on the Power Off button.

- Open the SD card cover and press lightly on the inserted SD card. Remove the popped-out SD card and close the cover.

- Insert the microSD card into your laptop or a computer.

- Create a separate folder and copy all the files from the microSD card into the folder. If the card is empty, skip this step.

- In the Drives folder on the PC/laptop, right-click the SD card, then left-click the Format command.

- Left-click the FAT32 option and left-click the START button.

- Eject the microSD card from the PC slot and insert it back into the tablet.

15.2 How to Delete All Data from Your SD Card

1. Swipe down and tap on the Gear icon to access Settings or hit the Gear icon on the Home screen. Tap on the Storage menu.

2. Under the SD card submenu, hit the Format as Portable Storage option.

3. Tap on FORMAT & ERASE.

15.3 How to Increase Storage Space on Your Tablet

Swipe down and tap on the Gear icon to access Settings or hit the Gear icon on the Home screen. Tap on the Storage menu. You have the following options available:

- Tap on the Internal Storage menu, and view the content categories (Apps & games, Miscellaneous, etc.). Tap on the category, then on the checkbox next to the content you want to remove. Hit the REMOVE button.

- Tap on the ARCHIVE NOW button under the 1-Tap Archive menu in order to remove the items not being used recently. The items stay accessible from the Cloud.

15.4 How Much Space is Left in the Internal Storage with All Pre Installed Apps?

With the apps installed by default, the amount of memory available to the user is 24.2GB. While some of the preinstalled apps can be deleted, there's no significant storage expansion available. An option to increase your storage capacity is inserting the microSD card. By that, you can add up to 256GB. The total available storage then is 280.2GB.

16. Alexa

16.1 How to Use Device Dashboard

1. Tap on the Smart Home button to the left of the navigation bar (on the bottom of the screen) or swipe to the center of the tablet from the bottom left corner on the lock screen. The Device Dashboard should appear.

2. Scroll down the screen to see all connected devices, their status, and any recent routines that have been applied.

3. Tap on the particular device you'd like to turn On and Off. You can also select turning all devices of a certain type (lights, plugs, switches) into the On or Off position, tapping the relevant buttons above the array of devices icons.

16.2 How to Solve Troubles Connecting Smart Home Devices via Device Dashboard

1. Make sure you can control your smart home device from your tablet. The following device types are compatible:

   - cameras

   - lights

   - thermostats

   - switches

   - plugs

2. Make sure the smart home device is turned on and working properly. For battery-operated devices, replace the battery with a new one.

3. Examine the smart home device's settings. It should be linked to Alexa and displayed in the tablet's Alexa app.

4. Ascertain that the smart home device, tablet, and Alexa app are all on the same Wi-Fi network.

5. Check if the Amazon account used on the tablet and for the Alexa app is the same one. The cameras and routine cannot be managed by the secondary profiles.

6. Ensure that the smart home device, tablet, and Alexa app are all running the most recent software version.

7. If a smart home device is hooked up through a skill, deactivate, and enable the skill again.

8. Turn off the parental control on your tablet.

9. Turn off and then on the smart home device after restarting the tablet.

16.3 How to Connect Smart Home Devices to Alexa

1. To open the Alexa app, tap its icon on the Home screen.

2. Select the three-lines button in the top left corner of the screen and tap on the Add a Device option.

3. Tap on the type of gadget you want to link.

4. Hit the device model name on the dropdown list.

5. Follow the on-screen guide to finish setting up your device.

16.4 How to Use Alexa on Your Tablet

1. Swipe down and tap on the Gear icon to access Settings or hit the Gear icon on the Home screen. Tap on the Device options menu.

2. Toggle the Alexa switch to the On position (the switch should turn orange) and Alexa will be enabled.

3. Hold the Home button (a circle on the bottom of the screen). If the Hands-free mode of Alexa is activated, you can say "Alexa" while the tablet is active. The blue line should appear on top of the bottom panel. Alexa cannot be activated if the tablet is in sleep mode.

4. Make a request (e.g. "Find the nearest barber shop", "What time is it", or "Turn on the light in the hall").

5. If you asked Alexa to play a video, audio, or read a book, you can ask to pause or resume the playback.

Things you can address Alexa:

- general questions

- search apps and options

- make shopping orders (if you've got the Amazon Prime subscription, your billing address is based in the U.S., and the 1-click payment is activated on your tablet)

- play video and audio (including the multi-room performance)

- read out the books

- manage the connected smart devices

16.5 How to Enable Alexa Hands-Free

1. To access Settings, swipe down and tap the Gear icon, or press the Gear icon on the Home screen.

2. Hit the Alexa menu and open the Alexa settings.

3. Tap on the switch next to Alexa to enable it. The switch should turn orange.

4. On the dropdown list, hit the Hands-Free Mode option.

5. Tap on the switch next to the Hands-Free Mode inscription. The switch should turn orange.

Tip: If your tablet is protected by a PIN or a security password, enabling Alexa may necessitate entering the PIN or a security password.

While the tablet is locked, you can disable Alexa Hands-Free activation by following these steps:

1. To access Settings, swipe down and tap the Gear icon, or press the Gear icon on the Home screen.

2. Open the Alexa settings by taping the Alexa menu.

3. From the dropdown list, select the Hands-Free Mode option.

4. Tap on the switch next to the Hands-Free Mode inscription. The switch is supposed to turn gray.

16.6 How to Permanently Disable Alexa

- Swipe down and tap on the Gear icon to access Settings or hit the Gear icon on the Home screen. Tap the Alexa menu and open the Alexa settings. Tap on the switch next to Alexa inscription. The switch is supposed to turn gray.

- Swipe down and tap on the Gear icon to access Settings or hit the Gear icon on the Home screen. Tap on the Parental Controls menu. Toggle the switch to the On position by tapping it (the switch becomes orange). Enter the password for your parental control in the drop-down window and then enter it again in the field below. Tap on the FINISH button below. Alexa will be blocked.

Note: Alexa cannot be removed from your tablet.

16.7 How to Use Fire Tablet Device Dashboard

- Turn on and off each smart home device connected and check its on/off status by tapping on its window. The following device types are compatible:

- cameras

- lights

- thermostats

- switches

- plugs

- You can turn on and off all devices in such categories as lights, plugs, switches. Tap on the relevant button (On or Off) below the inscription "All switches" or "All lights", etc.

- Scroll to the bottom of the screen and tap on the routine to view it.

16.8 How to Switch to Show Mode

- Swipe down on the tablet screen and open the Quick Settings menu. Tap on the switch next to the Show Mode to the On position. The switch is supposed to become orange.

- If Alexa is enabled, you may ask it to turn on Show Mode. Say, "Alexa (or "Amazon", if you've chosen that wake word), turn on Show Mode."

17. Data Reset

17.1 How to Factory Reset Your Tablet

Hold the Power button (at the right-hand side) for 3 seconds or until the tablet turns off. If the notification message appears on the screen, tap on the Power Off option.

1. Open the SD card cover and press lightly on the inserted SD card. Remove the popped-out SD card and close the cover.

2. If your tablet isn't locked:

   - Swipe down and tap on the Gear icon to access Settings or hit the Gear icon on the Home screen.

   - Tap on the Device Options menu.

   - Select the Reset to Factory Defaults option.

   - Tap the RESET button below.

If your tablet is locked and you can't unlock it or turn it on:

- Hold the volume button down and the Power button at the right-hand side simultaneously and hold it until the reset screen appears.

- Hold the volume button down and up to access the Wipe Data/Factory Reset option.

- Press the Power button and open the confirmation window.

- By pressing the Volume button (up or down), choose the option Yes, and then press the Power button again.

Tip: The factory reset operation removes all inserted data and app-related purchases from your tablet.

17.2 How to Soft Reset Your Tablet

1. Press the Power button at the right-hand side for 20 seconds or until the tablet shuts off. If a notification message appears on the screen, tap the Power Off option.

2. Wait for 5 seconds, then press the Power button again for 3 seconds, or until the tablet turns on. The Soft Reset is completed.

17.3 How to Reset Lock Screen Password or Parental Controls PIN

1. Ensure the tablet's Wi-Fi connection is activated and has no issues.

2. If you remember the password/PIN:

   - Swipe down and tap on the Gear icon to access Settings or hit the Gear icon on the Home screen.

   - Tap the Security & Privacy submenu.

   - Select the Lock-Screen Passcode option.

   - Enter your current PIN or password.

   - Enter the new PIN or Password, then fill it in again in the field below.

   - Tap FINISH.

If you don't remember the password/PIN:

   - On the locked screen, fill in the wrong PIN or password five times. The notification window appears.

- Tap on the Reset Your PIN option.

- Fill in the password for your Amazon account and hit the CONTINUE button below.

- Fill in a new Password or PIN, then fill it in again in the field below.

- Tap FINISH.

18. Ads

18.1 Where are Ads Usually Shown?

- When the tablet isn't in use, it appears on the lock screen.

- Pop-up advertisements are a requirement in the description of both free and prepaid apps.

- When you start the video applications, you'll get prime video recommendations for automated playback.

18.2 How to Remove Ads from Your Tablet

#1 Make a one-time payment:

1. Go to the Amazon web page for managing content and devices on https://www.amazon.com/mycd.

2. Log in using your Amazon account data.

3. Tap (if you do it from a tablet) or click (if you use a computer) on the Devices tab and find your tablet on the list. Tap or click on it.

4. Find the Special Offers submenu and click or tap on the Edit option.

5. Hit the Remove Offers option.

6. In the popped window, view the price for the ads removal and tap or click on END OFFERS AND PAY THE FEE button. An email notification will be sent to you.

7. Hit the CONFIRM button to pay the fee and disable lock screen ads on your tablet.

#2 Address the Amazon Customer Service:

1. Call Amazon Customer Support at 1-206-922-0880 (for US citizens/residents) or fill out the Customer Support form on the Amazon website: https://www.amazon.com/gp/aw/contact-us.

2. Request that advertisements be removed from your device from the Customer Service Agent. You may leave your request on the following grounds:

   - the active Amazon Prime subscription

   - the device is more than 1 year old

   - the option Special Offers is not available in your Amazon account settings

#3 Use Ad removal tools:

1. Swipe down and tap on the Gear icon to access Settings or hit the Gear icon on the Home screen. Hit the Device Options submenu.

2. Tap several times (up to 10 times) on the Serial Number digits to disclose the Developer Options menu.

3. Tap on the Developer Options and find the Debugging submenu. Under this submenu, hit the switch next to the Enable ADB option. The switch should turn orange.

4. Connect the charging cable's USB Type-C connector to the appropriate slot on the side of your tablet. Connect the USB Type-A connector to the computer's (with Windows 8 and higher OS version) appropriate slot.

5. Check the computer's Drives folder to see if the tablet is listed under the My PC menu.

6. Install the software for removing Amazon ads. Ensure the software source is reliable.

7. Unpack the software on the computer and run it.

19. Common Tablet Problems & Solution

19.1 How to Fix Massive Battery Drain Issue

1. Press and hold the Power button at the right-hand side of the tablet for 40 seconds or until the tablet shuts off. Allow 60 seconds to pass. Press and hold the Power button again for 3 seconds or until the tablet restarts.

2. Find the draining app. There are two ways to find out which app causes the battery drain:

   - Swipe down and tap on the Gear icon to access Settings or hit the Gear icon on the Home screen.

   - Hit the Apps & Games submenu.

   - Hit the Manage All Applications option. A list of all the apps installed on the tablet will appear.

- Tap on the apps one-by-one and hit the UNINSTALL button on the right, then tap OK. Do this until the battery drain stops.

- Save your files to the microSD card or another external storage and then reset the tablet to factory settings (refer to the **"How to Factory Reset Your Tablet"** section of the manual).

- Open the Cloud storage or run the Amazon Appstore and start to install the apps one by one until the battery drain is detected.

3. Access the Task Switcher (the square icon on the bottom panel) and dismiss the apps you don't need right now. Swipe the relevant windows to the sides.

4. Tap on the switch next to the Low Power Mode to activate the power-consuming mode (the switch turns orange). Tap on the Automatic Low Power Mode submenu. Tap and drag the circle on the slider to establish the battery level at which the battery-saving mode will be activated.

5. Turn off the tablet when it's not in use. Press and hold the Power button for 40 seconds or until it shuts off. If a notification window appears, tap the Power off option.

6. To limit internet access during idling periods, enable the Automatic Smart Suspend mode (refer to the **"What is Smart Suspend?"** section of the manual).

7. Enable Airplane mode to shut off the connection through Wi-Fi. Swipe down on the screen and tap on the airplane icon to turn on Airplane mode. The icon should change color to orange.

19.2 How to Fix eBook Disappearing Issue

Enabling Whispersync feature

1. Make sure your tablet is connected to the internet via Wi-Fi.

2. By pressing the browser icon on the Home screen, you can open the internet browser.

3. Proceed to the Manage Your Content and Devices page.

4. Enter your account information, then tap on the CONTINUE button.

5. Tap on the Devices tab.

6. On the list, select the name of your tablet.

7. Tap the Settings tab to access the tablet settings.

8. Find the Device Synchronization (Whispersync Settings) option and tap the switch next to it. The switch should be in the On position.

9. Return to the Home screen by pressing the Home button (the circle icon on the bottom panel).

10.   Swipe down on the screen, the dropdown menu opens.

11.   To enable synchronization of your tablet with the Cloud, press the Sync button (the two circular arrows icon). The Sync button should change color to orange.

12.   Hold the Power button for 40 seconds or until the tablet turns off. If a notification window appears, hit Power Off. Wait for 20 seconds and long-press the Power button again in order to restart the tablet.

Clearing cache on the Kindle app

1. To access Settings, swipe down and tap the Gear icon, or press the Gear icon on the Home screen.

2. Hit the Apps & Games submenu.

3. Tap the Manage All Applications option. The tablet will display a list of all the apps that have been installed.

4. Locate the Kindle app and tap its icon to open its settings.

5. In the app settings menu, hit the FORCE STOP button.

6. Hit the CLEAR CACHE button.

7. Hold the Power button for 40 seconds or until the tablet turns off. If a notification window appears, hit Power Off. Wait for 20 seconds and long-press the Power button again to restart the tablet.

Solving the Google Play Store issues

If you installed the Google Play Store on your tablet, the apps present in both the Amazon Appstore and the Google Play Store might work incorrectly.

1. On the Home screen, find the Google Play Store app and tap it to open.

2. Tap the bar on top and type the "Kindle" word.

3. On the dropdown list, find the Kindle app, and tap on it.

4. Tap the Uninstall/Delete button.

5. In the confirmation window, hit the Uninstall/Delete button again.

6. Tap the left-facing arrow at the bottom of the screen to get the main screen of the Google Play Store app.

7. Hit the icon with your account in the top right corner of the screen, then tap the Settings option.

8. Tap the downward-facing arrow next to the Connection Settings menu. A dropdown list appears.

9. Hit the Auto-Update apps and open the submenu.

10.   Tap on the circle icon next to the Do not auto-update apps option. The circle is supposed to change the color to green.

Tip: You can still update each app manually after disabling auto-update in the Google Play Store. Find the app in the Google Play Store and tap the green UPDATE button next to it.

19.3 How to Fix the Stuck Kindle Logo

1. Make sure your tablet's battery is fully charged.

   - Connect the USB Type-C cable to the USB Type-C slot on the tablet, then plug the adapter into the wall outlet.

   - Wait for at least 15 minutes for a tablet to charge.

   - Without detaching the USB cable or removing the adapter, press and hold the Power button until the tablet turns on.

   - If the tablet restarted successfully, and the battery charge is above the middle level, remove the USB cable from the slot and the outlet.

2. Check if the tablet is recognized by another device.

   - Connect the charging cable's USB Type-C connector to the appropriate slot on the tablet.

   - Connect the USB Type-A connector to the computer's appropriate slot.

- Open the My PC menu and locate the Fire drive.

- If the Fire drive isn't recognized, contact Amazon Customer Support at 1-206-922-0880 (for US citizens/residents) or fill out the Customer Support form on the Amazon website. If the tablet is recognized by the computer, unplug the USB-C cable, and restart the tablet.

3. Perform the Factory reset.

- Press the Power button for 40 seconds or until the tablet restarts. If a notification window appears on the screen, hit the Power off button.

- Wait for 20 seconds and press the Power button again until the tablet turns on.

- If the screen with the Kindle logo gets stuck again, press simultaneously the Volume button down and the Power button for several seconds. The Recovery menu should appear on the screen.

- Navigate via the Volume button on menu options to get to the wipe data/factory reset submenu.

- Hit the Power button. Pay attention that this action will remove all the progress in the apps, the installed apps and personal files, as well as the data of your Amazon account. Apps and files that have been downloaded to the Cloud can be re-downloaded.

19.4 How to Fix Constant Shutting Down Issue

1. Ensure your tablet's battery has enough charge level.

   - Connect the USB Type-C cable to the USB Type-C slot on the tablet, then plug the adapter into the wall outlet.

   - Wait for at least 15 minutes for a tablet to charge, but better leave it plugged in until the battery is full.

   - Disconnect the USB-C cable and see if the shutdown issue had been removed.

2. Restart the tablet.

   - Hold down the Power button for 40 seconds or until the tablet turns off.

   - If the notification window appears on the screen, hit the Power Off button there.

   - If the tablet doesn't restart automatically, press and hold the Power button for a few seconds until the screen lights up.

3. Check your screen timeout settings.

- Swipe down from the top of the Home page. Open the Settings by tapping the small gear in the bottom corner of the window (or go to the Settings menu on the Home page).

- Tap the Display option, then on the Sleep menu.

- Tap the circle next to the longer timeout option (e.g. 1 minute). The circle should change its color to orange.

4. Examine the potential sources of overheating.

- Remove the case, if any.

- Press the Power button until the notification window appears or the tablet turns off. In the notification window, tap the Power off button.

- Place the tablet in a cool and dry place for 30 minutes.

- Turn on the tablet by pressing the Power button for 20 seconds or until the screen lights up.

5. Perform a Factory reset.

- Make a copy of your files and send it to the Cloud, or connect the tablet to the computer and create a reserved folder for your tablet.

- Activate the factory reset of the tablet. Refer to the "**How to Factory Reset Your Tablet**" section of the manual.

6. Contact Amazon Customer Support at 1-206-922-0880 (for US citizens/residents) or fill out the Customer Support form on the Amazon website.

19.5 How to Fix "An Internal Error Occurred" Problem

1. Ascertain that the tablet's Wi-Fi connection is active and that the network is accessible.

2. Swipe down on the screen, tap the Wi-Fi button to deactivate it, and then hit again to activate Wi-Fi.

3. Keep an eye on the number of bars present on the Wi-Fi icon. If there are three or fewer, try connecting to a different network. If the Wi-Fi signal is weak, come closer to a router or restart your Wi-Fi router device.

4. Hold down the Power button for 40 seconds or until the tablet turns off. If a notification window appears on the screen, hit the Power Off button in the window.

5. If the tablet doesn't restart automatically, press and hold the Power button for a few seconds until the screen lights up.

6. Swipe down and tap on the Gear icon to access Settings or hit the Gear icon on the Home screen. Hit the Apps & Notifications submenu.

7. Tap the Installed apps tab. Find the app that is displaying the internal error notification in the dropdown list and select it.

8. Tap the FORCE STOP button, then CLEAR CACHE, and CLEAR DATA buttons. When the notification windows appear, tap the OK button.

9. Swipe down and open the Settings menu (or from the Home page). Tap on the Device options submenu.

10. Select the Date & Time submenu. If the box next to the Automatic time zone is empty, tap on it to put a tick there.

11. Check the time reading at the top of the screen to see if it shows your local time. If not, enter the correct readings. For that, refer to the **"How to Set or Change the Time"** section of the manual.

12. Deregister the tablet (refer to the **"How to Deregister Your Tablet"** section of the manual). After the procedure is completed, re-register the tablet with your Amazon account.

19.6 How to Fix Overheating Issues

It is normal for the tablet to warm up slightly while in use or during the charging process. You may experience overheating issues if the tablet becomes uncomfortably hot.

1. Make sure the tablet is well ventilated. If the tablet has been in a case, remove it and place the tablet in a cool, well-ventilated area. If possible, place the tablet onto a tablet stand in the vertical position.

2. Check what internal process causes the overheating. Swipe down and tap on the Gear icon to access Settings or hit the Gear icon on the Home screen.

3. Hit the Apps & Games submenu.

4. Hit the Manage All Applications option. A list of all the apps installed on the tablet will appear.

5. Tap on the apps one-by-one, and hit the UNINSTALL button on the right, then tap OK. At least make a 5-minute wait before uninstalling the next app. If the tablet cools

down during that time, the uninstalled app was most likely the source of the overheating.

6. Save your files to the microSD card or another external storage device and perform a factory reset on your tablet (refer to the **"How to Factory Reset Your Tablet"** section of the manual).

7. Open the Cloud storage or run the Amazon Appstore, and start installing the apps one by one. At least make a 5-minute wait before the installation of the next app. If the tablet cools down during that time, the uninstalled app was most likely the source of the overheating.

19.7 How to Fix Battery Charging Issues

It takes about 4 hours to charge the tablet using the wall adapter. A full charge via the USB-C cable plugged into the computer could take up to 14 hours. If you use your tablet while it is charging, the process may take longer.

1. Check if the USB Type-C port is working and the USB-C cable isn't damaged.

   - Connect another USB-C cable and the wall adapter to your tablet and see if the charging starts/becomes faster. It is recommended that you use an Amazon-certified USB-C cable and wall adapter.

   - Connect the charging cable to another device that supports the USB Type-C connection and see if the charging starts/is performed at the normal charging rate.

2. Charge in the non-active state.

   - Turn off your tablet by holding the Power button for 20 seconds or until the tablet shuts off. If a notification window appears on the screen, tap the Power off button.

- Insert the USB-C cable into the USB-C port on the tablet and plug the wall adapter into the outlet.

3. If the tablet's light doesn't turn on when the charger is hooked up, try mildly pushing the USB-C connector into the port.

4. If the charging doesn't start or is performed at a slow rate, contact Amazon Customer Support at 1-206-922-0880 (for US citizens/residents) or fill out the Customer Support form on the Amazon website.

19.8 How to Fix an Issue with a Sound Not Coming Through Speakers/Headphones

1. Ascertain that the volume is within your hearing range.

   - Press the Volume button up. The volume slider should appear on the screen.

   - Tap and drag it up on the screen or continue pressing the Volume button up.

   - Swipe down and tap on the Gear icon to access Settings or hit the Gear icon on the Home screen. Hit the Sound submenu.

   - Set all switches to the On position (the switches should change color to orange) by tapping on them.

2. Soft reset the tablet.

   - Connect and disconnect the headphones to/from the 3.5mm port on the right side of the tablet.

   - Press the Power button for 20 seconds or until the tablet turns off.

- Wait for 40 seconds, then press the Power button again to turn on the tablet.

- Run any voice/music/video app and check if you hear the sound.

3. Slowly jiggle the headphones' jack in the port while having the headphones on. If you hear the sound or static and/or the noise, the 3.5mm port requires fixing. Contact Amazon Customer Support at 1-206\-922-0880 (for US citizens/residents) or fill out the Customer Support form on the Amazon website.

Made in the USA
Las Vegas, NV
01 December 2022

60758425R00095